FOR THE PLEASURE OF PEACE

FOR THE PLEASURE OF PEACE

Transformative Listening in Marriage & Relationships

CHANA RACHEL FRUMIN

MSC CNT

ISBN: 978-965-599-215-1

For more information, additional copies or to contact Chana Rachel Frumin, please write to: Chana.frumin2@yahoo.com

CONTENTS

בס"ד

Rabbi Zev Leff

הרב זאב לף

Rabbi of Moshav Matityahu
Rosh HaYeshiva—Yeshiva Gedola Matityahu

מרא דאתרא מושב מתתיהו
ראש הישיבה—ישיבה גדולה מתתיהו

D.N. Modiin 71917 | Tel: 08-976-1138 טל' | Fax: 08-976-5326 פקס' | ד.נ. מודיעין 71917

Dear Friends,

I have read portions of "For the Pleasure of Peace" by Mrs. Chana Rochel Fruman. Mrs. Fruman is a long time acquaintance of mine who is an accomplished therapist. I am familiar with a number of people she has helped and she has had a positive effect on the lives of many people.

Mrs. Fruman presents a course of action to be used by couples to work out their differences and achieve "Sholom Bayis", marital peace and harmony. The ideas are well thought out and seem to be a reasonable method.The presentation is accompanied with case histories and practical advice on how to implement the ideas presented. I have not found any idea presented not in line with Torah Hashkafa.

I commend Mrs. Fruman on a quality presentation and pray that the Almighty bless her and her family with life, health and the wherewithal to continue to contribute to the community.

Sincerely,

Zev Leff

Rabbi Zev Leff

Dear friends: I've had the opportunity to read portions of Chana Rachel Frumin's book *The Pleasure of Peace*. Although it is short in length, it is full of potent ideas and practical advice for a successful marriage. Basing herself on decades of work as a therapist, she backs up her ideas with real case histories, showing easy to understand solutions for even the hardest marital challenges. At the beginning of the book an easy to remember paradigm is presented and then elaborated upon in a very down to earth and applicable manner throughout the book.

I highly recommend *The Pleasure of Peace* and congratulate Chana Rachel Frumin for her important contribution in making good marriages an attainable reality.

With blessings for success,

Avraham Arieh Trugman

Rabbi Avraham Arieh and Rachel Trugman, Directors

Moshav Mevo Modiim, D.N. Hamercaz, Israel 73122
Tel: 972-8-926-5247 Fax: 972-8-926-5448 E-mail: trugman@netvision.net.il www.thetrugmans.com

Dedicated with endless love and appreciation to

Zusha

My husband and best friend

Also dedicated to

Tammy and Simcha Edell

Who save lives and who saved mine

With gratitude to my friends
Chana and Matisyahu Rosenblum
May they be blessed

Hillel says: "Be among the disciples of Aaron, loving peace and pursuing peace..."

—*Ethics of the Fathers* 1:12

INTRODUCTION

Sometimes, problems simply cannot be worked out. Sometimes, the differences between people defy making sense of situations. However, this does not mean we need to end a marriage. We can transcend these differences, moving onward and upward without working them out.

(Please forgive the provocative nature of this idea until you finish reading this book, which is the product of a ten-year-study in co-creating successful marriages without working everything out.)

In our society, many things move too quickly. Food is fast and music is faster. News travels around the world at the touch of a button. And relationships end just as quickly, sometimes also at the touch of a button. There is great richness in creating a relationship that lasts a lifetime. Sometimes that is achieved not by working things out, but by transcending the problem. To do that, we need to create a way of being and a way of loving that protects a couple from the ravages of misunderstandings and mistakes.

By now you may be thinking that there must be some

mistake—don't people *have* to work through their problems in order to achieve a harmonious relationship? That is what many people—including many counselors—think.

This little book is here to present a completely different perspective. Let's start by considering the problems with the model of "working problems out." First of all, sometimes there is no middle ground—she loves the action of the city and he loves the song of the crickets in the country. They might decide to buy a second home, but there is no way they will be able to live most of the year in both the city and the country. Other times, the problem may get resolved, but we still don't feel at ease. Even years after a problem has been dealt with by a couple, one of them may bring up the old event to prove a point, or emphasize what they have been putting up with. Or perhaps lines were crossed and an apology was given. Yet, aying "sorry" is often not enough, since it fails to provide solace or a solution. Even when trust needs to be rebuilt, even when mistakes need to be forgiven, even when problems are unsolvable, there is a different way a strong marriage can be built.

A friendship can be created that will bring pleasure to the marriage, and joy and stamina to the partners. This friendship is so satisfying that, regardless of any problems or mistakes, the couple chooses to carry on and grow together.

Before you give up on your relationship, I would like to suggest that you try creating what I call, "The Way of Peace."

I have taught this system to thousands of couples and can attest to the fact that it works.

Even if your relationship is good, it can be deeply enrich through this unique approach. In this book, I will teach you the skills to grow closer and to develop peace, pleasure, and friendship through the creation of personal peace. The skills involved are simple: honoring and caring, being fascinated by differences, romance, peaceful diversity and respectful negotiation. With just some thought and practice, peace is within your reach.

ACKNOWLEDGMENTS

I would like to thank my seven children, who inspire me every day of my life, and fill my heart with love.

I offer deep appreciation to Rav Zev Leff, my rabbi of 40 years, who opened my heart to the Jewish world.

Thank you to Peter Kline, who was like a father to me, and to Charles Fauteu, my first great teacher in counseling.

To Michael White, who loved mankind and opened for me the doorway of enlightened counseling.

To David Epston, a therapist of miracles and caring for humanity.

To Dr. Annette Lavovitz, a master historian and storyteller.

To Hemla Levitt, who taught me about unconditional love.

To the greatest group of caring professionals I ever worked with: Rabbi Chaim Tabasky, Shlomo Zalmon Jessel, Batya Jacobs, Ruth Sager, Rafael Nathan, Binyomin Weiss.

To my greatest work partner, David Kaufman and his wife Daniella, who are both true healers.

Much gratitude to my dear spiritual family: Rabbi

Avraham and Rachel Trugman, Shmuel Moshe and Menucha Rothenberg, Dolev and Zahava Gilmore, Chaim and Judy Rosenblum, Zev and Linda Korn, Simcha and Tammy Edell, Michael and Michal Oshman, Chaia Gilbar, David Dilman, and Solomon Sikirdji.

Much thanks to Eliyahu Berkowitz for the marvelous writing skills he brought to this project, and to R. Eliezer Shore, for his expertise in writing and publishing.

L.E.A.R.N.

We are going to learn a practice of making peace, creating peace, and establishing peace instead of focusing on your needs, or your rights, or who is right and who is wrong. It is a daring adventure in building a new marriage that is more resilient and more pleasurable than other focuses and… it works to create a relationship that can last forever.

I will be using the acronym LEARN.

LEARN *is a helpful acronym for remembering a communication style that can bring personal peace and pleasure into relationships. It is useful in all interactions.*

LEARN

L = **L**isten.

E = The language of **E**ncouragement.

A = **A**ppreciate the other culture.

R = **R**omance and **R**espect.

N= **N**egotiate, ask for what you want or need, granting freedom for "yes" or "no," as well as being able to share your own ideas!

LEARN is an approach to relationships that creates both

inner peace and pleasure between people—replacing competition, tension, anger, and resentment.

LEARN is also a way of living that keeps marriages fresh by preventing stagnation and boredom.

When we **LEARN**, our focus is clean of heavy emotions and, instead, is filled with fun, adventure, and newness.

Chapter One

FOCUS ON WHAT YOU WANT TO GROW

Focus, like water, makes things grow. Practice focusing your thoughts on the positive elements of your life and relationship—on the things that you want to see grow. Begin creating Personal Peace by closing your eyes, taking a deep breath, and envisioning one of your spouse's characteristics that warms your heart. Think of an experience where you witnessed your spouse demonstrating this virtue.

FOCUS GONE WRONG

Frequently, a critical voice took over Moshe's thoughts, convincing him that his life was a disaster. He felt he had no control over his life or over the dialogue of negativity that filled him with darkness. Much of what this voice focused on was his wife, Margot. The empty space between him and her began to fill with tension. Then, gradually, when the tension grew unbearable, Moshe began to make subtle comments, tiny complaints about her. Sometimes they were justified by a grain of truth, but more often than not, they were trivial things that could have been ignored or allowed to slide.

Eventually, the many possessions lying around the house reminded him that her mere presence irked him. If she made a meal, it was badly prepared. Her singing as she walked around the house—a habit that Moshe used to find so attractive—now grated on his nerves. Moshe soon felt that everything she did was a dart aimed to strike him. So, he began to strike back, criticizing whatever Margot did do and complaining about whatever she did not do.

Margot became aware that what began as a lull in a conversation had turned into a prolonged silence, which eventually grew into an angry monster. The anger had taken on a life of its own; it morphed into a creature that entered their home uninvited—separating them and threatening their marriage.

When the silence and anger became unbearable, Margot and Moshe sat down and spoke, finally putting what they both knew into words. It was difficult at first and some hard truths were shared, but they agreed that there was still love. Something had to be done about the anger that had come between them, making it impossible to see the love they knew was there. This angry presence, which we named "The Voice," was so pervasive that it had become a part of their lives, a third partner in the marriage, a massive barrier that stood between them. Margot was ready to do anything to get The Voice out of their marriage. The reason for naming the threat they were facing was to encourage the couple to become a team to stand against this negativity. In Narrative Counseling, this practice is called "Externalization." It reflects the core belief that people are not their problems. People are separate from their problems and therefore can completely change their relationship to a problem. Externalization enabled Moshe and Margot to join forces. It was no longer husband versus wife; they now became a team, proactively defining the relationship they would have with that angry Voice. Let's listen in on how their conversation went....

To begin, I asked Moshe, "What is The Voice trying to prove?"

He knew the answer right away, since The Voice had been drumming the same message into him for so long.

"The Voice is saying that Margot has serious problems that need to be fixed," Moshe said. "It's telling me I shouldn't put up with these problems!"

"Has the criticism worked to diminish the problems?" I asked. "Does The Voice help the problems go away? Does it make your life better?"

"No," admitted Moshe. "It... The Voice... actually makes the whole situation worse. The Voice doesn't fix the problem, but The Voice won't go away, so I have no choice but to live with The Voice and live with the problems. Sometimes I feel like nothing will ever change no matter what I do."

"Why do you listen to it? What power does it have?" I asked.

"Well..." Moshe considered, "The Voice is right. The house is a mess. Margot spends too much. There are so many problems. There's no end to the problems."

"Does The Voice tell you that criticism will solve these problems?" I asked.

Moshe thought. "No, The Voice doesn't tell me how to fix it. And I know complaining won't help. But what else can I do?" Moshe asked in frustration.

I turned to his wife. "Margot, do you have any ideas what else Moshe could do?"

Margot considered. "I want to discuss what is bothering Moshe, but there is no way I am going to go on living with The Voice standing between us. It has taken me some time to realize that this Voice seems to have a will of its own. The Voice tells Moshe to only see the bad things, the things that annoy him. And The Voice makes all the problems look bigger, until all Moshe can see are the problems. That makes the entire situation worse. I am a very busy mother. In addition, I am taking care of Moshe's elderly parents. It is a lot for me, but I am happy to do this for him. I just want Moshe to notice these things, and not only the problems."

"What would that give you?" I asked.

Margot breathed a sigh of relief. "If Moshe focused a little bit on those things, on the good things I do for him, then I would be able to hear it when he tells me what he needs in other areas."

Gradually, the marriage changed. Little by little, Moshe learned to focus on Margot's efforts to look after their six children. He also saw how his wife was giving him the valuable gift of caring for his elderly parents. The more he focused on these things, the more significant they grew in his eyes. He expressed his gratitude more, whereas Margot, now feeling secure and appreciated, was able to listen to his sensitivities, whenever she could. Eventually, he was able to ask for a tighter spending plan in a manner that Margot actually appreciated.

Even his vocabulary changed. He began to ask, "Is this possible?" rather than, "Why don't you ever think about this?"

When Moshe changed his focus, he saw Margot's accomplishments. The Voice continued to point out the difficult things, but it was no longer the boss. Despite The Voice, he was able to continue in his new approach to speaking with Margot. This new approach brought positive results for both of them.

FOCUS GONE RIGHT

The foundation of a good marriage, and indeed of every good relationship, is focus.

Whatever you focus your attention on grows stronger. Focus is an awesome tool that is available to every human being. In essence, focus allows a human to do, think, or imagine anything they hope for at any time. This is the first step in bringing our desired goals into existence. When we harness this extraordinary human ability—the ability to choose our focus—we can make a plan about what we want to have in our life. Children are very familiar with the power to create reality through use of focused imagination. Adults are as well, but in a more practical manner; we do this by making a plan and focusing on it. That plan becomes the fabric of our life, though it begins as a picture that exists only in our mind.

Planning is a necessary part of everyday life. When it comes to relationships, however, many people claim to prefer a relationship that is not preplanned—one that just flows naturally. In truth, a natural, flowing relationship can also be the result of a plan, and such relationships are usually more successful than unplanned ones. Planning provides a framework for the natural flow to occur. It creates a space for people to come together. Without planning, the meeting may not happen, or it may happen in a harmful manner.

Most people suffer from some degree of selfishness, anger, and thoughtlessness. If you live only according to your natural inclinations, these harmful traits tend to emerge more often, becoming a bigger part of what you have to live with. However, if you actively use focus to rise above your basic nature, you begin to speak a different language, with words that move you forward in your chosen direction. Your actions will also begin to change. Focusing gives us the ability to transcend personal weaknesses. Instead of repeatedly falling into undesirable patterns of behavior, you can focus on something new: a new way of responding, or a different way of positioning yourself in relation to "the Problem." This new idea, when put into practice, can lead you to create a different life for yourself, with different people in it, or to seeing the same people (including yourself) in an entirely new context.

A STORY OF CHANGING FOCUS

Pam spoke of not getting her needs met in her marriage, and I asked her what this meant to her.

"What does getting your needs met have to do with marriage?" I asked.

"Why else would people get married?" she asked in return.

"Can you imagine any other reason? Why else might someone get married?" I asked.

This opened a new line of thinking, and she began to discuss the idea of companionship. She had never considered companionship as a valid reason to get married. It seemed like an "old-fashioned" concept.

I asked her to describe companionship.

"Well," she considered. "It's about two people hanging out together and just living with each other's problems."

We discussed her thoughts about the fairly modern idea of "getting one's needs met." I asked her if a marriage based on need fulfillment was a better marriage, one that had fewer problems.

"Marriage doesn't always go so well when needs are the focus," she admitted. "For one thing, needs cause resentment. Like, why should I have to meet your needs, especially if you haven't met mine? Also, why should I spend my life meeting your needs? My life should be about meeting my own needs."

I asked Pam what her needs were.

"I need the freedom to work and to have friends," she stated. "I need to be appreciated by my husband. I need to be seen and told that I am beautiful and intelligent."

I asked her how that was going.

"My husband is not so attentive," she admitted, "Also, when I take too much freedom, he's not so happy either. We spend a lot of time dealing with resentment, and that means my needs are not really being met."

She realized that when her focus was on needs, her marriage was lacking, leaving her unsatisfied and angry.

"What would your marriage look like if you focused on companionship, instead of on getting needs met?" I asked.

Pam thought a few moments before replying. "He is a really good companion," she said. "He is gentle and kind. We also have fun together."

Suddenly, because of her shift in focus, rays of sun began to break through the clouds, and her marriage could begin to grow.

Pam recognized that there was more caring and affection between them when she was not focused on her needs. She appreciated the caring as much as she wanted her needs to be met.

FOCUS CAN CHANGE THE "BIG PICTURE"

Life can be exciting and wonderful—a truly joyous gift. But, it can also contain pain and confusion. When a person focuses on the points of pain in life, they start to believe that everything is about pain. They no longer see the light and happiness that is also there, mixed in with the pain. This influences their actions and their outcomes. This is how focus becomes a self-fulfilling prophecy, and takes on the appearance of inevitability.

When the focus is on pain, pain is all that you are able to see. Of course, the natural reaction to pain is to become tense and edgy. So, if that is all you can see, all of your actions will follow suit. Rather than allowing you to cope with the pain, focusing on the pain will continue to bring even more pain into your life. Even if there is a period without any pain, you may not even notice it, because you are so busy focusing on pain. Or, you may notice, but consider it only a temporary phase, as you continue to anticipate the pain you are sure will reoccur at any moment.

This constant focus on pain blocks out the ability to see anything pleasant or sweet, even when it is in front of your eyes. When you control your focus and direct it toward what is good, you will be able to see the goodness you were unable to notice before. Naturally, this will also cause you to create even more good. When you are not focused on pain, yet something painful happens, you will be able to perceive it as an isolated incident, or as part of a larger experience that contains some good. You will not experience the bad as a monolithic expression of your entire life.

When you change your focus, you effectively change your entire world; you purposely obscure the bad by overlaying it with good.

In a marriage or any close relationship, focusing on kindness and compassion keeps the relationship filled with light. In this way, it is possible to overcome personal difficulties and create a connection that is a blessing to both partners. The raw materials for happiness are already present in each of our lives; they are just hidden from sight. As it does in many areas of life, lack of focus causes us to become distracted from the true qualities with which we want to fill our marriage.

Indeed, a lack of focus allows weakness to take over.

Human nature must be refined in order to create a space for peace and happiness. Left unrefined, human nature invites selfishness, coarseness, jealousy, anger, and lethargy. When human nature is polished, you can expect to see optimism, charity, kindness, and compassion!

It is commonly agreed that planning and focus are essential tools when it comes to finances and saving money. Careful planning allows for other things to become possible. For example, it can provide financial security for your children, as well as enable dream vacations to happen. Spontaneity is exciting, but the tool of planning brings a different, potentially more powerful kind of excitement into your life.

This can also be clearly seen in the way many people relate to food and time. Food and time are two major aspects of life, yet many people have an unstructured relationship with them. This leads to undesirable consequences. When meals remain unplanned, junk food easily takes the place of a healthy diet. Refrigerators remain empty, people snack all day, and family no longer share mealtimes. Eating with focus and intention means planning meals, sitting down when we eat, and focusing on the experience without distractions. Eating with a loved one reinforces the experience, loading it with meaning. Mealtime creates a sense of bonding and belonging, even more so if the meal is simple and positive. Although food plays the central role in mealtime, food alone does not make a meal. Group meals are significant and remain in people's minds—not only because of the quality of the food, but also because of the atmosphere and the shared experience. Yet, such meaningful and healthy group experiences rarely just happen. They require planning, from the shopping list and cooking, all the way through the cleanup and refrigeration of the leftovers. Nevertheless, the spirit of togetherness and rich memories that family meals create are well worth the investment.

Living without a plan leads to a life full of unpaid bills and missed appointments. When time is a planned experience, the house gets cleaned, errands are taken care of, and most days run according to a smooth schedule. Lack of focus means your time is filled up with things you don't want, rather than things you do. You are so busy reacting to whatever comes your way and catching up that you never take the time to have fun. Conversely, focusing solely on spontaneous fun and "going with the flow" means that matters of importance fall by the wayside. Without focus, something important will always get left out.

The same is true in relationships. The tool of focus makes time spent together an intentional and exceptionally deep experience. When time is intentional, you can plan a year ahead, a month ahead, or a week ahead. This means that you can include in your life everything that is meaningful and essential to you and your spouse.

A MEDITATION TO IMPROVE FOCUS

- Sit in a comfortable position.
- Close your eyes.
- Concentrate on your breathing, deep and slow, as you listen to the sound of your breath.
- Envision your loved one sitting with you. Envision them smiling at you, giving you a gift.
- If a distraction enters your mind, envision a gull swooping down and plucking the thought up and carrying it away, disappearing into the distance.

FOCUS EXERCISE

Some people find it helpful to see a physical reminder. Start out by writing a one- or two-word name for your focus goal on a piece of paper, like "Appreciate," or "Show love." The description can be as general or as specific as you like. Every time you actively focus on your goal during the course of the day, make a plus sign on the paper

If you like computers, send yourself a letter each day detailing one step you took toward achieving focus in your relationships.

FOCUS: A SUCCESS STORY

Every day, Rachel's father burdened her with criticism. He thought that criticism was essential for her to grow into a thoughtful and refined woman. This constant flow of judgment was injected into every aspect of Rachel's life: how she dressed, how she ate, her friends, and how she behaved with the family. There wasn't a single area of Rachel's life that was safe from his withering criticism.

During her teenage years, Rachel internalized her father's critical attitude, making it her own, and incorporating it into everything she did. She focused the judgment inward. It filled her thoughts and influenced her actions. She continued on where her father had left off, criticizing every aspect of her own life, always finding things about herself that were lacking. This focus on her own faults became so destructive that whenever Rachel had a disagreement with anyone, it would end with a need to punish and, sometimes, even hurt herself.

To the casual observer, Rachel was impeccable in every way. She dressed neatly, presented herself in a poised and elegant manner, and made a positive impression wherever she went. She pushed herself to exceed in gymnastics, a sport she loved, and worked hard to perfect her moves and routines. If she failed to execute a move perfectly, however, she would spend hours steeped in bitter anger, until she came up with some "appropriate punishment."

This focus on self-loathing was a secret, known only to Rachel herself. One day, Rachel fell in love with Michael, an intelligent and well-mannered man. At the top of his class and an officer in the army, he was known for performing charitable acts. They seemed well-suited for each other. Rachel was as beautiful as he was handsome. They were both talented in academics as well as music.

Then, there came the fated day when Rachel and Michael disagreed about a very important topic, as every couple will do at times. Rachel slipped into the old patterns she had learned from her relationship with her hypercritical father. She became passive, ceding victory without attempting to express herself, and canceling herself out of the relationship. In the aftermath, she sank into bitter self-loathing, searching for a proper punishment to give herself for being inadequate.

Michael witnessed this dramatic change and called off the relationship, declaring there was no room for such extremes in his life. Rachel was heartbroken. She had no healthy tools to overcome such a loss.

Rachel began therapy. When I asked what led her to seek help, she answered that she was "too intelligent to end her life, which is the only fitting punishment for losing the relationship with Michael."

Therapy was exceedingly difficult for Rachel. Dealing with problems was acutely painful for her. Together we explored what it would mean for her *not* to be perfect. We discovered that the need for perfection was part of her relationship with her father, expressed through daily criticism. Even though Rachel's relationship with her mother was nonjudgmental and supportive, it could not counteract the power of her father's daily criticism.

As we explored her life and those areas that were not perfect, gradually a notion arose that Rachel had not encountered in her childhood. The idea was that there could be more than one perspective in life; that there are multiple ways of perceiving the same thing. A transformation slowly started to occur. Rachel invented what she called the "Maybe Game." This game became her stand against perfectionism.

The "Maybe Game" became Rachel's way of staying in the moment. Whenever a topic or an opinion made her question her worth, she immediately told to herself that this was only one perspective. The Maybe Game allowed her to focus on the possibility that there might be an alternative perspective, a different way of perceiving the situation.

The answer could be one thing or another. Perhaps there were several equally valid ways of seeing the problem and, maybe, there was even a yet unknown solution. The situation was not black or white, and she might, or might not, be to blame.

This shift in focus moved Rachel into a new way of experiencing and accepting her life, whenever she felt that she was imperfect.

Not long after we ended our sessions, Rachel sent me a letter describing her new experience:

DEAR CHANA,

How are you? I hope you had a good trip and that you're enjoying the summer with your family.

I wanted to ask you if you happen to know of a nutritionist whom you could recommend. I thought you'd be a good person to ask, since you're into health food. I was lacking a bit of energy at gymnastics, so my coach suggested that I might need to gain weight and wants me to see someone about it. This was actually a great "Maybe" story, because my first reaction to this suggestion was to think, "No, I don't need to!" Then I started to get all upset, thinking, "What if there really is a serious problem?" But then I told myself, "Maybe it's worth looking into. I'll ask a nutritionist, and either she'll tell me everything is fine or she'll help me improve my eating patterns. It can't hurt." I was really proud of myself for being able to accept advice in an area that I consider so personal.

I had another good "Maybe" story, too. A friend sent me an email that I was offended by. Instead of writing an angry reply, I wrote down my feelings to myself. Then, after a while, I responded to the email expressing my hurt, making it about me and writing in a friendly, understanding way, without accusing. And guess what? I got an apology and it didn't create hard feelings between us! I celebrated that one and wrote it down in my diary as a major success, because usually, such a thing would be difficult for me, but I did it. I was so excited!

I also wanted to share with you my experience with the "Maybe Game" during our visit to the United States: I noticed a lot of criticism among my extended family, which made it even more of a challenge to focus on the positive. It also helped me feel a little more understanding toward my father, because he grew up with a much higher degree of criticism than what he raised us with. It hasn't changed my relationship with him, but it still showed me something illuminating.

Shabbat Shalom and thank you so much.

P.S. I also wanted to share some exciting news with you: I'm dating a new boy. So far, we've gone out three times, and I haven't heard a single critical remark from him about anyone! He must be a member of the anti-criticism society!

A CLOSER LOOK AT THE "MAYBE GAME"

To cope with her inner feelings of judgment, Rachel created the "Maybe Game." This game enabled Rachel to shift her focus away from criticism and focus on seeing at least two possibilities in each situation. In the game, aspects of her life didn't have to be judged as perfect. While playing this game, she was able to overcome the destructive voice of perfectionism and focus on other voices that described her life.

When she dated a man, she asked him if he would be willing to learn this game and play it with her. Today they are married, and she tells me that he is better at playing the "Maybe Game" than she is. As Rachel put it: "Married life is good—the 'Maybe Game' continues to help us focus on the right things, understand each other better, resolve disagreements, and just relax!"

LISTENING

FOCUSED LISTENING VS. FILTERED LISTENING

The act we call *listening* is most often not pure listening; rather it is a process of filtering what we hear. We are bringing in some of what is being spoken and discarding the rest. This is not real listening. Real listening is the process of creating a space of acceptance and nonjudgment in order to welcome another person's thinking and culture. We have been trained to listen in a busy way. Sometimes we are taught that always being mentally occupied is a sign of intelligence. So, we are intelligently listening by busily filtering everything we hear. However, there is an entirely different practice that not only uses intelligence but also sensitivity and compassion. It is called focused listening. It offers the speaker a sense of being valued and of belonging in the world.

CASE STUDY: WHEN LISTENING DOESN'T HAPPEN

Ed and Ann were married many years. They had three children: nineteen-year-old Miriam, sixteen-year-old Mark, and fourteen-year-old Shoshanna. Ed had a problem with anger management. Their family life was frequently disrupted by his screaming and throwing insults at everyone. He also demanded a lot from his family, and criticized everyone. frequently. He was unhappy about how his family was turning out, and stated this often. He blamed his wife for all of this, saying he only lost his temper because of her. The children, however, felt unsafe around him and related to their mother as an ally. When Miriam turned nineteen, she decided she would no longer speak to her father.

Ed and Ann decided to come for counseling. Ed expressed how he felt unheard and unimportant in the family. He claimed that Ann laughed at him and told stories about him to their children. He felt that she did not respect his boundaries and did whatever she wanted.

For her part, Ann had grown tired of being yelled at, and did not take what he said to heart. She considered his frustration to be his problem, independent of their relationship, and attributed it to his frustration with his job. Whenever Ed expressed his opinion, Ann would respond by saying his fear and insecurity were taking him over.

Ed felt increasingly isolated and alone within his family, which led him to yell even more. Ann felt that Ed was terrorizing them and that he cared only about his own needs. Things were difficult all around.

One day, they joined another family and some friends for a vacation. When it was time to return home, Ann wanted to put six people in the car for the return trip. Ed was adamant that this was illegal and dangerous. Ed insulted Ann in front of the others, expressing how careless he felt she was to bring up this idea. When no one took him seriously, he felt that he was not being heard and began to yell. The situation quickly went from bad to worse.

It was clear that Ed and Ann needed to begin listening to

each other. More than that, they needed to appreciate what the other had to say and to let the other feel this appreciation. As a couple, they had lost all interest in hearing from one another, and listening to the viewpoint of their spouse. The children had become part of this pattern, as well. It hurt Ed terribly that his children were rejecting his relationship with them.

In desperation, Ed decided to change. As a result of learning about focus, he decided to focus on listening to what his family was saying and what they needed. He explored expressing his needs gently and respectfully. This replaced his usual tactic of yelling and demanding to be heard. As Ed softened, Ann began to share her personal ideas and insights with him. When she felt listened to, she began to trust his perspective and be open to his needs. In response to Ed's listening ear, Ann did her best to listen to him in return.

Ed and Ann focused on asking each other questions to fully understand the other's opinion. Gradually, they began to listen for hints of depth and sensitivity. Sooner than they could have imagined, their marriage was back on track.

LISTENING CAN GIVE OR TAKE AWAY VALUE

When someone is motivated to listen because they are truly interested in the other person and in building a relationship with them, the experience is filled with comfort and is uplifting for the speaker. This type of listening creates a rich experience of thinking and sharing that allows personal growth to happen. When I feel listened to I gain a sense of belonging and I feel valued—a profound experience!

The ideal in a relationship is for listening to serve as a framework for coming together, growing together and understanding each other. When you understand someone, you serve them by giving them support. This makes the speaker feel valued and offers both people a sense of feeling cared about.

Being empowered in this way is a rejuvenating experience. It affects the way a person thinks about their lived experience. Real listening literally opens up a new way of seeing life and of making sense of it. Truly listening to another person sparks connection and helps them feel loved. This kind of listening leaves behind a mutual feeling of warmth and vitality.

CASE STUDY: LISTENING AS GIVING

John and Amy had been married for ten years. Amy was a strong-minded and beautiful woman. John was a gentle and intelligent man. Whenever they were in the company of another couple, John could not handle how Amy smiled at them and listened intently to whatever they were saying.

"You value them more than me, John would complain. "You never listen to me this way. Our marriage would be great if you would agree with me the way you agree with them!"

Amy responded: "But they're discussing thoughts and ideas that have nothing to do with me. You always talk about my life and how I'm doing. You always criticize me and tell me how I should change. I'm not into listening to that—I want to be accepted for who I am!"

John tried again: "You're my wife, and when I'm with you, you need to think about what I need. That's what a wife is supposed to do for her husband. It makes me very sad that I can't get your help and attention!"

"The truth is," Amy countered, "that you think only about yourself. You don't even notice how hard I work and how much I do for the children. Why can't you get your mind off your own needs and be more present?"

These conversations would drag on and on, and end up reducing both Amy and John to tears. Then they wouldn't speak to each other for a couple of days, until they were finally and reluctantly able to begin a discussion about what needed to get done. Both of them were quite closed when they came in for counseling. They didn't really want to speak much, and yet they were so unhappy that they thought they'd better try.

I began by introducing them to the importance of real listening: "You know, in the wintertime, we wear coats, but when we enter a house, we take the coats off. I'm wondering if you can both 'take off' the complaints about the communication problems in your marriage and try a new kind of interaction. I'm suggesting that the new mode of communication not entail what you think your spouse is doing wrong, rather, it will focus on the many positive things you think about your spouse and about your life together. Later on, you can focus on how to ask for what you want. For now, we are exploring what it is like to share your life and your stories, simply because it is fun to have a companion."

This was unfamiliar territory for Amy and John, and at first they found it difficult to put aside their pain and complaints. They began by limiting themselves to whatever they could say that was interesting or appreciative. Within a few days, they already felt better about each other; they were both surprised that speaking in this kind of way had such an immediate effect on their relationship. Speaking in order to share rather than to rebuke, and really listening to each other, changed their feelings about one another. They would never have guessed it was possible, without having to solve every problem they were facing!

INSTITUTIONALIZED LISTENING

Some people listen in order to feel more powerful and important than the person they are listening to. This is called "one-upmanship." It is a practice that sociologists have explored, and have found to occur in the majority of human interactions. This type of listening often occurs in institutions, and often makes the person being listened to feel controlled, drained, and isolated. The underlying message is that the speaker is not very smart, and has very little value to the listener. Sometimes, this listening is about feeling right or correct at the speaker's expense. The listener feels powerful and important because they are the "go-to" person and the final authority. This type of listening serves as leverage to exert power over the speaker, as if to say, "The proof that I am more important than you is that you need me to listen to you!" Clearly this is a subtle, yet most uncomfortable experience. In an unspoken way, I devalue the person I am listening to. Even though some listening is taking place, it can be a damaging experience, as well.

There is a concept in psychology that human beings can suffer from a "want of power," and a desire to feel greater than someone else.

Power is a force that requires a person or an object to exert power over. One might think that this is the appeal of power —to be able to control things, to change them to fit one's vision of reality. (This can obviously be good or bad, depending on who is in power and what their vision is.) But a more recent idea suggests that people who desire power are mostly looking to control one thing—themselves. This presents two different conceptions of power—power as influence and power as autonomy. "Power as influence is expressed in having control over others, which could involve responsibility for others," Julie Beck writes, in an article in

The Atlantic. "In contrast, power as autonomy is a form of power that allows one person to ignore and resist the influence of others and thus to shape one's own destiny."

INSTITUTIONS

In institutions, the function of listening as an act of one-upmanship serves practical purposes, yet it comes at a high price. Schools, hospitals, law enforcement, and even corporate structures operate on hierarchies, which encourage a type of listening that includes one-upmanship, with the boss listening to his subordinate in order to grade the latter's performance, or a professional listening to a client to get the facts that they need to take some action. Here, communication becomes a presentation and the speaker is judged on his performance. Although essential to the running of these institutions, hierarchical relationships should be viewed as necessary evils, since they assign value to members—raising some up at the expense of others, and leaving others entirely outside, with no value in the hierarchy. Whoever is left out will struggle to find a sense of self-worth. If they are unsuccessful, their search for value may take them in destructive directions. That is why such listening has no place in our homes, among our nearest and dearest.

Institutional listening is a form of filtering, which means that the listener is waiting to hear certain kinds of information. This might be information they agree with, or even information they disagree with. Sometimes, filtering is in order to gather relevant information, or to give advice. Institutional filtered listening has become the most prevalent way that people communicate with each other today, and we have all become accustomed to it. Yet, it can have the effect of shutting down communication even during attempts to communicate. The speaker feels pigeonholed or boxed-in by this experience, because things that are important to him are being filtered out. The speaker feels misunderstood, used, or taken advantage of. Filtering is often what we do in place of listening. The question then becomes, when are we filtering and when are we really listening?

Filtering is a legitimate approach to listening in most social situations, such as in business and in education. But, filtering sounds the death knell for intimate relationships. Filtering is not the full experience of listening needed for deep relationships. It leaves the listener and the speaker divided and even unrelated, turning a relationship into a power game.

Ideally, listening should create a connection, a sense of belonging, and enhance a fuller understanding of another individual. As Michael White, co-creator of Narrative Counseling, put it, "Listening is about being human together." This deeper kind of listening empowers the person being listened to. When the speaker is empowered by feeling thoroughly heard, he feels valued and united with another. When we are listened to, we walk away with a sense of purpose and happiness. Feeling purposeful is one of the ingredients of happiness. This practice is beneficial for the listener as well as the speaker. This kind of listening builds a better world and energizes both the speaker and the listener. The listener shows he appreciates the value of the person he is listening to, which adds value to his own life, as well. Taking the time and energy to listen in this manner is difficult, but it is an investment that quickly pays off. Every word you hear and every response you offer is another brick in the palace of your relationship, creating a uniquely precious space for friendship and intimacy.

CASE STUDY: UNFILTERED LISTENING AFFECTS THE LISTENER

Early in my career, I worked in a Youth Service Bureau. I was assigned to a class full of teenagers who had been removed from the regular school system. They were being allowed to spend their time in school so that they could receive a degree while, in fact, they were learning nothing. They were sweet and misguided children, who gradually began to fall into crime and drug use to get their minds off their experience of failure and isolation. For a full year, I taught them meditation and communication skills. We built a relationship where they were given the chance to speak and the affirming experience of being listened to with interest. Everyone in the group was taught to listen and then reflect back what they heard. They also were asked to share their thoughts regarding what they found interesting about the topics being discussed. Slowly, each child grew more interested in the speaking as well as the listening part of this experience. We discussed issues like integrity and morality, as well as dreams and feelings they had about their lives. Many of these young people had never before been listened to in this deep and accepting way, and they began to abandon their previous lifestyle. By valuing each other's ideas and activities, through unfiltered listening, they grew positive and purposeful. Through this new pattern of listening, they acquired new self-worth and were able to leave behind years of hierarchical listening that had left them feeling worthless and uninteresting as people.

DECENTERING: A DIFFERENT EXPERIENCE OF LISTENING

We live in a very competitive society. The contest begins when we are young children in school, in classrooms that are focused only on the smartest. The teacher asks, "Who knows the answer?" and everyone jumps to raise their hands. It is a contest. Children who lag behind are ridiculed, labeled and ignored.

We are educated to focus on getting the point quickly and giving a brief response to prove that we are smart and worth doing business with. This "me in the center" approach becomes the model for our personal lives as well. Even in friendships and marriage, when we should be taking time to see the big picture and the whole person, we are still waiting to jump up and raise our hands with the right answer. We are trained to listen for "the point" and no more.

But what (barely) works in the classroom and the workplace spells death for a relationship. If a conversation with a spouse becomes a classroom exercise or a standardized test—where we expect the right answer to pop out so we can get a good grade—then, listening becomes impersonal, standardized, and goal-oriented (with the goal being focused on "myself").

Ideally, listening should be a deeply personal experience. You need to hear the entire voice, understand the meaning behind the words, and hear the deeper messages. It is the very opposite of a standardized approach. It is the most personal experience possible, where one can express a lifetime of experiences from their own individual perspective. This creates a possibility of real closeness, understanding, and friendship.

This type of listening requires a state of openness. It means setting the world aside, closing the door to space and time, and focusing on the person and what they are saying. This is necessary in order to be entirely receptive to the world of your friend, spouse, or child.

Michael White called this practice "Decentering."

Decentering is a practice that creates space for two realities to coexist. By placing all of your own ideas and experiences to the side, you now have room to explore the world of the other person. You can appreciate the alternative impressions without requiring them to be like your own.

Decentering is not submission. You do not erase yourself or your beliefs. Decentering is an experience of two worlds, both of which have importance. By placing my world to the side, I can hear about your culture from a position of honor and appreciation. This experience in no way makes my life less important. It is like two books on a shelf, where both will be read, in due time.

CASE STUDY: DECENTERING IN ACTION

I was working with a charming young woman named Susan. Unfortunately, Susan was haunted by nightmares and frequently woke up in the middle of the night sobbing. She was sleep deprived and spent much of her day thinking of killing herself.

Years earlier, when I was a young therapist, I had interviewed many teenagers who were considering suicide. As a result, my sessions with Susan began to make me uncomfortable, as I was taking her threats seriously. I began to argue with her, pleading for her to choose life. Naturally I wanted her and all my clients to choose life over death, but in the process of trying to save Susan from herself, the listening part of our sessions got lost.

I decided to take this up with my supervisor. During the supervision, I was taken back to my earlier experiences. By speaking about the role suicidal fantasies had played in my early work, I was able to place it in a secure compartment of my personal history. Once I closed that door, it no longer interfered with Susan's therapy.

When I returned to my work with Susan, I was able to decenter and make a space to truly "hear" her story. The result was immediate. She told me that she had never been able to speak about this with anyone, because people were always trying to save her. She stated that what she needed was to have some time to talk openly about the subject. Our sessions were finally providing her with that space. She was now able to talk through her thoughts about suicide without outside influences. In the end, she realized that suicide was not the answer; what she needed to do was understand her nightmares, which we explored together.

MEDITATIONS FOR LISTENING

Stage One: Listening Meditation

- Sit comfortably in a quiet outdoor spot.
- Breathe deeply.
- Listen to the sound of your breath. Do this for five deep breaths.
- Listen to all the sounds around you. Do this for five breaths. Notice what happens to your feelings as you listen.

Stage Two: Hearing the "Other"

- Ask a friend to have a conversation with you, to help you become a better listener.
- Hear the tone of the speaker's voice.
- Notice the pace of the speaker's words.
- Open yourself to their lived experience, and acknowledge any additional messages contained within the way they speak.
- Let yourself respond with acceptance of whatever feeling or experience they are expressing.

LISTENING EXERCISE

- Sit with a friend while they relate a recent experience. While they speak, open your heart and "listen" to their story in order to appreciate their way of looking at life. Join them by taking a true taste of their experience.
- Practice seeing things from their perspective. Picture yourself growing smaller while imagining the speaker with a golden aura, growing stronger. While you take in their words, create an imaginary space, a large hall, that is a special place to store and treasure the words of the speaker.
- Practice responding in a way that focuses on them. Engage them with interest and curiosity, without your life or your values interfering in the direction of the conversation. When your own ideas pop up, ask the ideas to wait for another day.
- See where this dialogue leads. What benefits came from being so wholeheartedly involved in the words of the speaker?

Chapter Three

ENCOURAGEMENT

"Courage, dear heart." —*C.S. Lewis*

Encouraging others is an important aspect of being part of a family, a group of people, and a community. Everyone is doing their best in this world, and sometimes, a kindly word of encouragement can help others realize that they are cared for.

The language of encouragement creates communication that is filled with kindness, courtesy, praise, listening and curiosity. It gives the person a sense of being valued and having importance. People will willingly draw you closer when you speak the language of encouragement, since you bring a positive experience into their lives. When words are used that show that you value the speaker, and when they are combined with a tone of voice that is open and inviting, with eye contact and a pleasant facial expression, the listener will feel encouraged. This language opens the door for the listener to respond with kindness, sensitivity, and good will.

CASE STUDY: ENCOURAGEMENT GONE WRONG

After Cindy and David were married, they moved into his community where he had many friends. David loved to tell her stories about the history of his community and detailed descriptions of all the people.

Both were in their mid-thirties, thought they were in no hurry to begin having children. They thought it would be best to give their friendship a chance to slowly blossom into a family. Sadly, their marriage got off to a rough start. Whenever David would tell Cindy a story about his friends and their exploits, Cindy would express her lack of understanding with a certain expression she had used all her life: "What are you saying?"

Every time David told a story and would wait for Cindy's response, it would invariably be the same: "What are you saying?"

These words greatly annoyed David. He would get a strained look on his face, his voice would rise in volume and take on a harsh tone. Eventually, he would insult Cindy. This pattern went on for months until open hostility developed between them. Cindy confided in a friend, who offered a useful insight: "What do you think David is hearing when you respond, 'What are you saying?' Perhaps he feels written off or insulted!" Cindy was surprised. When she listened to his stories there was so much that she literally did not understand. She wanted to gain an appreciation for a culture that was greatly different from her own. When she realized that he might be hearing this as a judgment, she decided to make a change.

Unfortunately, Cindy forgot the earlier conversation and found herself, once again, listening to David tell a story about his friends. And once again, the words left her mouth: "What are you saying?"

Cindy saw the distressed look on David's face in reaction to the familiar phrase. She realized they were about to fall into the old pattern of confrontation, when she suddenly thought to ask: "David, what do you think I mean when I ask, 'What are you saying?'"

David screamed out: "You're calling me an idiot, like I don't know what I'm saying. I'm just as intelligent as you are, but clearly you don't think so!"

Cindy was speechless for a few moments. She had no idea that for three years this is what her husband had thought. She cried out, "That isn't what I mean at all! It's just an expression I used growing up. It means, 'Wow!' or 'That's interesting and I don't understand all of what you are saying.' David, I'm interested in what you are saying and want to get a clearer idea of why this is important to you!"

David and Cindy sat together in silence, saddened to think they had spent three years fighting over a complete misunderstanding. They agreed that in the future, before arguing, they would ask the question, "What are you hearing me say right now?" They understood that it would take some time to get over the pain, but they were amazed at how wrong they had both been about each other.

ENCOURAGEMENT: MORE THAN JUST WORDS

Words create worlds! They are powerful and can create worlds of meaning. Words are intended to convey a complete message, but they alone cannot accomplish this. Tone of voice, facial expression, the look in one's eyes—all come together to create a complex and unique message. Verbal communication, in all its complexity, is the diplomat or messenger, carrying our thoughts into the world, paving the way for what we welcome into our lives, and what we bring into the lives of others. The nature of our language either invites or inhibits a response. Manipulative or discouraging words invite one kind of response, whereas honest, encouraging speech elicits an entirely different one. When I choose to use a language of sensitivity and peace, my words take on a certain form.The language that we speak in our marriage invites many things that fill the spaces between two people. A colleague once said, "Don't let rudeness into the guest room of your life. The guests on your invitation list should be: courtesy, closeness, and goodwill, not resentment, confrontation, and rudeness." When words are spoken with good intentions, the significance of what we say is multiplied and increased. Rabbi Shlomo Carlebach (1925–1994) was a famous singer, rabbi, and spiritual leader whose influence and popularity is felt until today. He taught that even a heartfelt "Good Morning!" can become a blessing, a gift, and something a person might remember forever. Simple words said with a world of meaning behind them can be massively significant. Indeed, small words can literally save lives.

HOW ENCOURAGEMENT SAVED A LIFE

Once a woman was thinking of ending her life. She called her friend and told her goodbye.

Her friend said four caring words: "We will miss you!"

These words literally gave the woman the strength and encouragement to find a new beginning, in place of a bitter end.

ENCOURAGEMENT IS CLOSENESS

When a person wants to use language to invite closeness, they choose words and tones that foster a deeper connection, and use eye contact to create that bond. Conversely, whether intentional or not, a person can choose a language that discourages and destroys closeness, by using their eyes and a tone of voice to say: "Stay away!" Sometimes, when a person speaks, they will raise their eyes to the sky. This can deliver a stronger message than the words that were spoken. All these aspects together form a "communication culture" that is unique to the individual. I can change the meaning of every word I utter, if I say it with hints of sarcasm or of love, of condescension or of care. No matter which words are used, if they are conveyed in a broken, negative manner, they may deliver other unintended messages, such as:

I want to control you.
I am desperate to feel more important than you.
Just agree with me...
Don't you dare argue or disagree with me!
This is a waste of my time!
Please make me feel like I have value.
Leave me alone!
You'll be sorry for what you're putting me through!

Though these may not be messages the speaker intended to convey, they are most certainly picked up by the listener. When "I love you" is said over the shoulder with no eye contact, it is a painful message to receive. Choosing to say, "Do this!" with no trace of politeness or gratitude gives a controlling message. A frown changes any message completely. Tension in the voice may be meant as, "I love you, so I won't get upset," but could be received as, "If I could, I would totally explode at you." You may intend one message, but without making a conscious choice to create a communication culture that will build and encourage the other person, an entirely different message can come across. The listener becomes confused by the contradiction between the content of what is being said and the way it is being expressed. If the communication culture, the larger message, is negative, then no matter which words are actually said, they will be received in a negative manner. If the overall message is insulting, controlling, or insensitive, then the listener has a choice to either stop listening, argue, or submit. None of these are good choices if you are speaking to someone you love.

ENCOURAGEMENT: SMALL, YET POWERFUL

Encouragement sounds like such a minor thing, yet it brings massive results. Encouragement isn't small, at all—it is strength-building and powerful. When you're encouraging, you're literally instilling courage. That's huge!

In married life there is one indispensable ingredient that can transform and inspire individuals, foster a positive attitude, build self-esteem and enhance relationships. That ingredient is encouragement.

ENCOURAGEMENT GONE RIGHT

Sherry is a doctor. She works hard and helps many people. She brings in a good deal of her family's income—but she doesn't discuss it, in order to not make her husband, Ben, feel less important. But Sherry is not so good at offering encouragement.

Ben is quiet and studious. He is a teacher and a scholar. He is working on his Ph.D. and is well aware that Sherry is the major breadwinner in the family. In Ben's mind, this is something they should avoid discussing, in order that it not become a problem. Though he was willing to marry a doctor, he did not understand how hard it would be for him to always have to face his wife's high-achieving talents. He is more of a slow mover and considers Sherry's life to be like thunder and lightning. Over time, Ben and Sherry grew further and further apart. They lost their way to intimacy and even to conversation. When they came in for counseling they had been living separate lives for several few years. Ben began by stating that he felt that Sherry judged him and looked down on him. As Sherry heard Ben's feelings, she realized he was probably right: she had been looking down on him, although she had never admitted it to herself. She never gave him a sense of encouragement about his life and his accomplishments, because she had been so involved with her own. She decided that she would try to be encouraging, and asked him what type of encouragement he would appreciate. This was the first time in their marriage that Sherry had asked Ben this question. Their life improved greatly as she began to show interest in his pursuits and achievements, while Ben began to express his appreciation for her great financial contribution. They lost their fear of hurting each other and began to speak encouraging words.

SPEAKING THE LANGUAGE OF ENCOURAGEMENT: A PRACTICAL GUIDE

Tip: When you speak with genuine sincerity, you get extra credit points!

Show Interest:

How was the test?

How was your day?

Offer Expressions of Hope:

Have a good day!

Do well on your interview!

Sleep well!

Compliment:

You will come up with an idea. You always do!

I could not have done this without your help!

I always feel safe when you're driving.

You look so handsome in that jacket!

Show Courtesy:

Please feel free to share with me.

Thank you for taking such good care of the kids while I was out.

Excuse me. I didn't mean to bump into you.

Ask Permission:

Can we sit down and discuss the money situation sometime soon?

Are you open to driving me to the event tonight?

Offer Statements of Endearment:

Hey, honey!

Oh, sweetie, I'm so glad to be home with you.

Find Physical Ways to Show Encouragement:

Make eye contact.

Give an encouraging smile.

Turn your body to face the other person.

Calm down and relax tense facial or body muscles.

Use a gentle tone of voice, no matter what you say.

AN ENCOURAGEMENT CHECKLIST:

- Did your words give support, confidence, or hope?
- Did your encouragement fill the other person with the courage to face the world?
- Was it given in the proper tone?
- Did you make eye contact?

- Was it sincere?
- Was it received and internalized?
- Did it make a difference?

A SUCCESSFUL MARRIAGE THAT LASTED FOREVER

Shoshana writes:

When we were first married, my husband said, "If there is anything you need from me or anything you want me to do, just say, 'Honey, could you please…' and I'll do it."

Unfortunately, I did not take his offer well. My mother was a working woman, and she felt courtesy was equivalent to stooping and bowing. Her motto was, "I don't bow to anyone."

What a mistake—her marriage was filled with anger.

When my new husband said this to me, I thought, "No way! I am not going to stoop."

So, for the first three years of marriage, we had a lot of fights. "Oh no, this is turning out just like my mother's marriage," I thought.

Then one day, I really needed his help with something,

So I remembered what he had said and I quietly used his script, "Honey, could you please ..."

That was all he needed to hear—the courtesy lit his fire, and he jumped to help me.

I thought, "What a waste of three years!"

So now I am sold, and my new motto is: *"Courtesy at all costs, in all cases."*

PLEASE BE POLITE

In today's world, there is a sad lack of social graces. Each day, it becomes more likely that we will experience rudeness in our social encounters rather than courtesy. Yet, each individual can also make a difference in this area. Each of us can change the world with a kind word, a smile, and a positive response to whomever we meet. This could become a wonderful challenge, to say something that shows honor and courtesy to each person we speak to today. If our focus is on giving encouragement, even when it doesn't come naturally, we will find the right words. By saying a good word wherever we go, we are offering a sense of self-worth to everyone we speak to.

The message we give when we are polite is, "You are worth being spoken to! You are precious!" The listener feels that you care, and can then appreciate their own intrinsic value so much more—thanks to the way that you make them a priority. The marriage dynamic should really result in an exciting interchange, as two different ways of experiencing life are shared. When you focus on giving encouragement, the other person begins to change. They feel important and valued, which brings out the best in people, even in times of anger. One spouse may say, "He yelled at me," and the other may claim, "She is trying to control me." There are many subtler "invitations" for anger and insecurity woven into the way that we speak to each other, which are hard to recognize. We can change all of those bad invitations in a profound way, by making a decision to be encouraging. With each sentence we say, we can send the message: "You are important to me!"

ASSESS YOURSELF

- If I am honest with myself, how encouraging am I, on a scale of one to ten?
- How can I become more supportive of others, in word and deed?

- What changes am I willing to make to become more encouraging?

ENCOURAGEMENT EXERCISES

Everyone is different and needs different sorts of encouragement. It can take time to figure out what emotional language the other person "speaks."

Some ways to offer encouragement include:

- Share encouraging words through a card or an email, rather than saying them out loud.
- Make a new person feel welcome in a group by introducing them to others. In that way, you invite them into your circle of friends.
- Give them a gift.
- Give them a hug.
- Focus on the person you want to encourage when you are speaking.
- Think of something you feel the other person is really good at, and compliment them specifically on that.
- Think of what it is that you find so amazing about the other person, and tell them about that.

TAKING AN ANTHROPOLOGICAL INTEREST IN YOUR SPOUSE

Although we tend to think of culture in terms of communities, ethnic groups and nations, each individual also has a culture all their own. In our quest to become better spouses, we would do well to become ardent students of the culture of our spouse. Just as anthropologists study patterns of behavior, norms, and values, so, too, will we study those aspects of our spouse that are unique to them, and, perhaps, foreign to us. But study is not enough; we also need to appreciate their culture. Appreciation means recognizing and enjoying the good qualities of someone or something else, as well as a full understanding of a situation. Combining study and appreciation will help us master this marriage-building practice.

APPRECIATION GONE WRONG

A woman entered therapy to speak about how to get closer to her husband. She complained about his inability to speak about emotions. "I am quite alone when it comes to my emotional life," she said. "I also don't like the way he spends his time. He helps other people excessively. I think he should spend his time in more productive ways."

A different couple is working in therapy to overcome their constant fighting. She says that he criticizes everything. "He criticizes the amount of food I buy. The way I clean or how much I clean. He even criticizes how I arrange Shabbat meals with guests. I can't win. I need compliments and affection, yet all I get is criticism." On the other hand, he says: "She over-spends without regard for our budget. She hardly ever cleans unless I plead with her. She invites so many people to our table I can't even think. It's a terrible burden on me...."

Appreciating someone else's culture might seem an odd way to focus on your partner—but it works!

Consider yourself an anthropologist for a moment, studying a culture that is entirely foreign to you, with its own language, values, and customs, completely different from your own. Now, imagine yourself as an anthropologist who has encountered a woman or a man in a foreign land. Social anthropologists seek to explore customs, economic and political organization, laws and conflict resolution, patterns of kinship and family structure, gender relations, childbearing and socialization, and religion. Cultural anthropologists, on the other hand, seek to understand and describe each culture in its own perspective. And spousal anthropologists (my own term!) study their spouse's culture and become an expert on their values, preferences, meaning and habits, without subjecting that culture to a judgmental analysis. Here is a perfect example:

"We had been married a few months. I was a very conservative voter, as my country's values were very important to me. As we were driving, my husband mentioned that he was planning on voting liberally. I slammed on the brakes and pulled over. I couldn't continue driving until I understood why someone as sensible as he was planned to vote liberally!"

The goal is to become an expert in whatever is important and special to your spouse, and to make pursuit of this expertise a lifetime endeavor.

Even though it is not always possible to give your partner what he or she needs, it is still a loving act to be sensitive to what they value. Think about this for a moment. How often do we take time to simply understand and appreciate the values of our partner, without being concerned over whether we agree or disagree? This is a very loving practice.

We also want to have an appreciation of the experiences that our spouses have gone through in life—what was difficult and why? What remains behind in their memories? We want to understand whom they have loved and what those people meant to them. We want to appreciate whatever inspires them. The goal of this inquiry is to give rich support to your spouse, based on knowledge, intimacy, sensitivity, and understanding. We want to develop a constant interest in the life of this person we are growing closer to. We want to gain expertise in their past history and present challenges. We can also develop an understanding of the dreams for the future that they hold precious.

Society today does not encourage taking a deep interest in one another. Most relationships focus on expedient communication and needs being met.

Developing closeness through appreciation requires intellectual and emotional interest in everything about our partner's life, until we know our spouses as well as we know ourselves. We can become sensitive to ideas that matter to them, and create a much more interesting life together as we do.

APPRECIATION GONE RIGHT

My husband grew up in California in the 1960s. He spent most of his time on the beach. He loves meeting strangers, he loves the ocean, and he loves the freedom that was part of that culture. When he entered retirement, he wanted to spend all of his free time on the beach. I felt uncomfortable at first. I was bothered by the image of so many people just lying around half-naked. However, the more often he went to the beach, the happier he became. I realized that he felt younger and healthier by spending time at the ocean. I have relaxed and grown less judgmental since I realized that in his culture, going to the beach is like going back home for a visit. Nowadays, I occasionally go to the beach with him. That way we share this experience and it brings us closer together.

Once we are on our way to becoming experts on our spouse's culture, the second step is to appreciate everything our spouse does as part of our lives. Have you ever noticed that in every experience there is always more than one perspective available? When we realize how many different ways there are to consider a situation, we can pick whichever focus generates peace and friendship, rather than one that creates hostility and resentment.

When a friend of mine became sick, the women in the neighborhood often came by to help her. Her husband also pitched in to do part of the housework that was usually not his responsibility. My friend was grateful when they did the chores that she could not do, however, she was resentful when they did the chores that she could do! Sometimes the neighbors or her husband would come over when she was sleeping and clear the table or sweep the house. Those were the few chores she was still able to handle. She forgot to be grateful for other people's kindnesses, when the chore was not one that she chose. In therapy, we discussed what it would mean for her to appreciate it all—every drop of help. She said that, ultimately, it would be quite relaxing!

A woman asked her husband to take over the chores while she traveled for a week. When she returned she was furious, because the chores had been done differently than she expected. She forgot to see what her husband had accomplished, because of the false expectations she had been focusing on! When she readjusted her "expectation scale," there was room for more objective observation and appreciation, and she realized that he had actually taken care of everything quite efficiently, while she was gone.

In every relationship, we are presented with a challenge: will we focus on "how things should be" (meaning, how I wanted it to be) or will we focus on some aspect of the person or shared experience that we can appreciate. There is always something to feel grateful for, some point of light. Adding appreciation to our daily communication makes us feel more grateful and encourages our spouse to give more, because they are being appreciated.

All I need is a good word.
Just say thank you, it's all I need to hear.
Please, take one moment to see the good.

Consider a married couple where the wife works full-time and the husband works part-time, perhaps because his business is much more lucrative than hers.

When he is home, he washes the dishes. She returns from a long day and walks into a clean kitchen. She remembers to appreciate this act by thanking him for his consideration. To some, his actions may seem like a given, since he works much less, but his wife doesn't take them for granted.

If she would walk into the house thinking, "He's home most of the day. He *should* wash the dishes," then she would fail to see his act as a generous one. Gratefully acknowledging his act transforms it into an act of giving and kindness. Both spouses can grow and a marriage can flourish when each one appreciates the loving acts of the other.

One factor that makes it more difficult to appreciate the other is gender roles in our society. If the wife is "supposed" to do the laundry, then how can the husband appreciate her? She is simply doing her job. Same holds true of a wife, such as when a husband does home repairs. Once we step away from "should" and "supposed to" we can appreciate every kind deed. We also have room to explore our gender expectations and those of our spouses. Gender differences vary according to age, culture and upbringing. This is a realm rich with opportunities for understanding each other.

> When he opens the door for me I feel so touched, like he is always thinking about my comfort.
> When she goes out of her way to make sure I feel well and brings me something to drink, I feel respected and happy.

These gender expectations are a matter of personal preference, and the only ones that are wrong are the ones that fail to take into account the way the spouse sees the practice. One woman didn't like having a chair pulled out for her. It didn't feel like courtesy to her, she felt babied. One man wanted to go to sleep without a big goodnight ritual. These well-intended gestures need to be discussed and understood in order to lead to peace.

We can also learn to appreciate the feelings and viewpoints of our significant other. We can be touched by how much they care about life. We can appreciate their religious sentiments, and political views. Our life together can be filled with expressions of appreciation. Even in areas where we are different.

I SEE YOU...

Many people complain, even when no benefit will come out of it, and even when it can cause harm. Language is free, and hearing our own voice can be reassuring. There are times when we speak in a nasty way about someone else, in order to entertain ourselves or feel better than other people. This is a destructive way to act in an intimate relationship, since it fills the environment with a negative energy. Nastiness and judgment erode feelings of safety and trust.

Appreciation means speaking about life and other people with an eye on what is positive, pleasurable and delightful. Life contains so many mysteries, good deeds and wonders—at least as many as there are things to complain about.

We can use appreciation of life to fill our intimate dialogue and refrain from a bitter view of people and situations. This is a vast subject, so we will conclude this chapter by wondering: Do we appreciate what appreciation can do for our marriage?

Can you imagine what your marriage would be like if you mainly spoke about the positive side of life, filling your conversations with sensitivity and appreciation for each other's culture, instead of criticism?

There is another side to the practice of appreciation. It is at simply expressed by the words, "Thank you." "Thank you" expresses the very important sentiment that one values and appreciates what the other person does for you. "Thank you" says "I see you. I notice your presence—what you do and say. And I appreciate all of this as well." Saying thank you does away with taking you for granted or not noticing the other. It stands against indifference and insensitivity. When used in its true form (not merely out of obligation), it is an expression of respect and appreciation to another individual (and simultaneously to all beings) for the kindness they have bestowed upon you. "Thank you" is one of those wonderful phrases people use to express a special gratitude. But there's often a lot more to it than those two words can convey. When it comes from the heart, from deep feelings and special thoughts, "Thank you" means so *much*. It means thank you for taking the time to show that you care.

Chapter Five

ROMANCE AND RESPECT

> Respect, which is also called esteem, is a positive feeling or action shown toward someone or something considered important, or held in high regard. It conveys a sense of admiration of good or valuable qualities. —*Wikipedia*

Respect is about treating people the way *you* would like to be treated; that is, in a way that makes them feel cared for and important!

RESPECT GONE WRONG

I once participated in an advanced week-long workshop for therapists, in South Africa. I waited three days to speak with the teacher, because I wanted to introduce myself to an individual whom I admired. Finally, as he was standing on the stage during a break, I approached him and said, "Hello, I love your work!" He answered angrily, "You are interrupting my conversation with this man," pointing to someone who was standing behind him, whom I had failed to see. I blurted out, "But I've waited three days to introduce myself!" He growled at me, "Well, too bad you didn't wait longer!" I was so frustrated. Later I found out that he asked the director not to invite me to the next workshop. How embarrassing!

I had hoped to thank him for his wonderful work and instead he thought I was being totally disrespectful. I apologized, and asked him if I could start again. What a sorry beginning.

RESPECT

Respect is a positive action shown toward others that conveys a sense of admiration and honor. Respect can also be a group of practices that gives a person a sense of being valued and cared for. We accomplish this by listening carefully and exhibiting consideration for their needs, not interrupting when they speak, showing interest in their viewpoint, and expressing an acceptance of the differences between us!

Respect can be shown by being polite, kind, interested and patient. Respect can also be shown by giving a person space and time and, sometimes, *showing respect means forgetting all about certain events that happened—so as to protect a person's self-respect*. This can be quite a provocative idea—that sometimes, even many times, the best direction is to simply let bad encounters go *and forget that they ever happened*. At times, offenses can be forgotten or "released into eternity" and there can still be great love without having to confront mistakes and bad times. Respect includes knowing when to release experiences and when to talk about them. Painful or frustrating events can be discussed, as long as your spouse agrees to it, and as long as the subject is presented with thoughtful language that focuses on what is important for you, rather than words that criticize your spouse for what he or she is doing wrong.

An example of this might be, "When we go out together

on a date, I would rather we don't sit near people we know in the restaurant, but sit alone together, if that's okay with you!"

This is instead of, "It was very thoughtless and selfish of you when we went out to dinner and you said hello to the Cohens and agreed that we sit with them, rather than sitting alone with me."

The first expression does not make anyone feel bad or put the blame on one's spouse; it just suggests what you would prefer and is much easier to listen to.

There are different cultural ways to show respect.

In the Jewish religious world, we stand up for a teacher or an elder.

In Chinese culture, people give a small bow to elders.

In American culture, men shake hands to show respect, or open a door for the person walking through. In certain places, taking your hat off or giving up your seat is a show of respect.

Respect conveys to a person that you honor and value them—that they have importance in your mind and heart. In a relationship, showing respect causes the other person to feel valued, brings out the best in them and helps them to act with more integrity. People like feeling valued, as it is uplifting and creates feelings of pleasure. Feeling valued also generates feelings of friendship and trust. These good feelings help people rise above little annoyances and enable them to look the other way when something goes amiss. Respect plays a more important role in establishing a relationship than needs and expectations. Showing respect is like an announcement: "Lets consider our well-being as a couple more important than what one of us is feeling. Let's always make it about both of us." In other words, showing respect is a shortcut to well-being.

RESPECT STARTS WITH SELF-RESPECT

Respecting yourself means defining and appreciating your own worth as a human being; for if you do not respect yourself, it will be harder for you to respect anyone else. So, respectful behavior begins with *self*-respect.

Self-respect includes knowing you have value. Before all else, you have value because you were created, because you are alive. This value is not dependent on anyone or any thing. You have value because you are you. You have value before you accomplish something and you have value after you accomplish it. By knowing you have enduring, nonnegotiable value, you will approach your own life and other people in a richer and more dignified manner. It is imperative to practice knowing you have value!

Self-respect is a skill which, like playing a musical instrument, requires practice. Also, as with an instrument, self-respect begins with rigid practice and then becomes quite creative and intuitive. One practice of self-respect is to affirm one's intrinsic value, as in repeating, "I have value. I am creative. I have importance, as do all people." Other practices of self-respect can include: having a dialogue with oneself about how one feels about life, such as by asking, "What are my feelings about this?" or, "What does this experience mean to me?" Through such exercises, we first befriend ourselves and then simply listen to our different responses with honor and acceptance. Affirmations are another practice of self-respect, such as by filling our time with self-talk like, "I am good, I do good, and I have done good. I am unique and have a special way of looking at the world."

Self-respect can also mean living according to ethics that are important to you.

RESPECT GONE RIGHT

My husband's brother came to visit. His lifestyle is wild, and his beliefs are so different from mine that I felt quite threatened. I feared him influencing my children in a dangerous way!

This was his first visit since we had been married and I wanted to show respect for the sake of my husband, even though I felt uncomfortable. So I made a plan.

I went to pick up his brother at the airport, and after greeting him I asked if we could have a discussion about my own values and how protective I was of my children. I asked him to please respect my ways while he was visiting. I took responsibility for my own lifestyle, and framed it as different from his, rather than painting one of us as right and the other as wrong. He agreed and his visit was uneventful. I was quite grateful for how reasonably he acted while he was with us and we all had a great time together.

RESPECTFUL PRACTICES

- Listen, by opening yourself to the other person's experience without judging or trying to help.
- Stop all other activities when she is speaking and make direct eye contact.
- Smile at him while he is speaking.
- Ask permission before you speak. Ask permission regarding things you would like to do.
- Use courteous expressions like please and thank you.

MEDITATIONS FOR RESPECT

- Think of three ways you can show your spouse that you value them.
- Close your eyes and focus on the actions she or he performs every day that you appreciate.

ROMANCE

Romance is an emotional feeling of love.

Romance is a natural human emotion.

Romance idealizes values and principles that seem lost in today's world of technology and instant gratification. It can be an old-fashioned experience of love that makes people sigh with wishful thinking, or it can be falling head over heels in love with another.

Romance is also a style of behavior and a group of practices that create attraction, pleasure, and even feelings of love.

The word romance developed other meanings, such as the early-nineteenth-century Spanish and Italian definitions of "adventurous" and "passionate."

ROMANCE GONE WRONG

My husband and I never get to go away together. We decided that for the upcoming three-day weekend, we would find a nice beach and camp there. We went shopping ahead of time and borrowed a good tent so the sleeping would be as comfortable as possible. Then, on the morning we were supposed to leave, he looked like he felt sick.

I asked him, "Are you feeling ill?"

"No," he murmured, as if he had no voice.

"Then what's wrong? You don't look well," I said in a

crabby voice. "We are supposed to leave in an hour and you don't look like you want to go."

"Want to know why?" he growled.

"Sure," I thought, "let's get it out into the open and then we can have some fun."

"Because," he continued to growl, "you need so much attention that I will be exhausted by the time we get back."

"So much attention?" I asked. "We barely see each other. We work separate hours, and anyway, what do you mean I need so much attention? Everyone needs some attention."

"Not everyone needs it all the time. Most people need it sometimes and then they need space sometimes. You never need space, you only need attention!"

We had begun an actual fight.

We were yelling and I was feeling uncomfortable.

"Okay," I huffed. "Let's stay home and you can have your space." And with that, I marched off.

Looking back, I realized that I could have learned something very important that day—something that was important to my husband. But I didn't learn anything—I was just angry.

I could have taken the risk of listening to what he was expressing as a statement of what he needed in order to feel loving. He needed to be together sometimes, and sometimes he needed space. It seems clear enough today.

But it was not clear then. Everything was dark.

Romance often means taking a risk. Even for a married couple, being romantic is taking a risk. And it is certainly a risk if you are still in the dating phase. The risk is that you will get no response, or even worse, be rejected. You might even get criticized for how you expressed your romantic feelings! Or, you might get a response which is apathetic.

Once, a woman said to me decisively: "Our marriage is

past the hugging and cuddling stage!" They were divorced two years later.

I remember thinking, *this is not about a stage, this is about romance!* Romance is a practice of love and intimacy. By practicing romance, love often grows.

Why take the risk, you might ask?

We take the risk because romance is an expression of what is unique in an intimate relationship. There is only one relationship where I can express romance openly! Romantic words make our heart tickle, and warm up our whole body. Only in intimate relationships can we hear words like:

Hey, gorgeous!
Hey, HOTTY!
You are so beautiful to me.
Sweetheart.
You are the man of my dreams!
Will you spend the rest of your life with me, please?
You are my soul!
You smell sweet.
I love you every day.

There are also expressions of romance that are unique in each relationship. I asked some of the people I work with for some unique expressions of romance in their relationships.

Here is what their love-language sounded like!

You look so beautiful when you are all muddy. (A gardener told this to his wife, while she was in the garden.)
You are my miracle!
You are not my number one, you are my only one!
Let's take a walk in the forest. You give me energy when I walk!

> You are a wash-and-wear kind of girl. (The husband meant that his wife was easy-going!)

Or the following story:

> We were dating and I was trying to set up one of my friends with one of his friends.
> "I don't know if he will be attracted to her," he said.
> I said, "You think life is all about attraction. How chauvinistic! Women have a heart and a mind, not just a body!"
> He looked at me and said, "Sweetheart, you know I think you are so beautiful!"
> I couldn't help smiling when I heard that.

One woman said that the most meaningful moment in her life was when she had just given birth. Her husband picked up the baby, smiled, looked her in the eyes and said, "Thank you."

ROMANCE GONE RIGHT

It was clear that he liked me. He really listened when I spoke. He took a lot of time walking me to work in the morning, as we both lived in a small community. But he still hadn't asked me out. We sat next to each other at dinners we ended up at together, but there was no follow-through. I was wondering what to make of all this, when one day he came to my house and knocked on the window.

I looked out and smiled.

"Hi," I said, "how are you?"

He was standing quietly. I wanted to give him space, so I just smiled back at him.

Suddenly, he said, "I am sorry that I am so bad at dating. I just don't know how to do this."

I said, "You're doing okay," and we both smiled. We have been married now for forty years! My understanding that he needed a lot of space and that he needed to go about dating in his own way made it all work out in the end.

PRACTICES FOR ROMANCE

- Hold hands.
- Take a walk under the stars together.
- Sing a favorite song together.
- Play a game—just the two of you.

MEDITATION FOR INCREASING ROMANCE

- Close your eyes and think of a characteristic of your spouse that you truly admire. Remember an experience where your spouse demonstrated this quality.

Chapter Six

NEGOTIATION

SETTLING DIFFERENCES AND GROWING CLOSER

Negotiation is a process by which compromise, innovation, or new agreements are reached, while avoiding arguments and disputes. Oftentimes, when there is a disagreement over one specific point, further disagreements can develop, leading to misunderstanding, arguments, resentment, or actual fighting. Such outcomes leave no space for negotiations. In these cases, the problem arising from the disagreement is worse than the disagreement itself.

This negativity can leave everyone involved feeling hurt, angry, and unable to work things out. It can also negatively affect the entire relationship of a couple, a company, or a country. The opportunity to negotiate and work out a collaboration between two people can be lost for an extended period of time, or even forever!

There is an incredible range of subjects that people disagree about, but only a small number of core reasons that people disagree.

- Disagreements can be caused by differing facts.
- Disagreements can be caused by differing definitions of words and situations.
- Disagreements can be caused by differing values; that is, people value and care about different things.
- Disagreements can be caused by failures in logic; both sides have fallacious reasoning.
- Disagreements can be caused by the default beliefs of humans beings. Each person has a different set of fundamental beliefs that are so intrinsic to their way of thinking that they don't even realize they are beliefs and not facts! These beliefs have different built-in assumptions, which can make it impossible to see someone else's viewpoint.

Self-interest can cause disagreements. It often happens that people's minds will make it hard for them to acknowledge the truth, because the truth has negative consequences for them. In short, your mind may not *let* you see the truth because it anticipates the negative consequences of doing so, and it is trying to protect you from them.

Disagreements can also be caused by jealousy, competition, feelings of personal insecurity, and other negative emotional experiences.

A husband and wife may disagree on many things, but they must absolutely agree on this: to never, ever give up.

NEGOTIATION GONE WRONG

Every war in history has been based on a disagreement that failed to be negotiated.

World War II was the deadliest conflict in human history, marked by eighty-five million fatalities.

The Empire of Japan aimed to dominate Asia and the Pacific and was already at war with the Republic of China in 1937. But the World War is generally said to have begun on September 1, 1939. This was day that Nazi Germany invaded Poland, which led to the subsequent declarations of war on Germany by France and the United Kingdom. When one country invades another, there is no hope for negotiations.

The war in Europe concluded with an invasion of Germany by the Western Allies and the Soviet Union. This culminated in the capture of Berlin by Soviet troops, and the unconditional surrender of Germany on May 8, 1945.

Millions of lives were lost and the only possible outcome was surrender. No negotiation was possible.

Many marriages are like war. They have no possibility of negotiation. Sometimes, they don't even have the possibility of surrender. Many divorces are like war. These situations leave many people wounded or destroyed.

Here is an illustration of failed negotiation on the home front, which, unfortunately, functioned as a battlefield as well...

A marriage failed. There were two children involved, ages four and six. The mother claimed that the father was abusive. She hired a lawyer and accused the man of child abuse. For the next two years, the father, Max, could only see his children once a week for one hour, in a room where he could be observed. Max was a devoted father and had never actually committed abuse. However, no proof was necessary in this legal system. If the mother claimed there had been abuse, she was believed. After two years, Max was allowed to spend two hours per week for the *following* two years. Finally after four years, Max was able to bring the children to his new home, as long as his new wife agreed to be the responsible observer of all interactions. There was no negotiation possible throughout the entire four years, just accusations and restrictions. In this situation, Max paid a painful price, as did his children. He was never proven to have hurt the children in any way. There simply was no proof.

NEGOTIATION SKILLS

It does not have to end this way. It is possible to conduct effective negotiations within a marriage.

Negotiating means asking for what I would like and for what would make me happy, while understanding that my marriage partner may not necessarily agree with my wishes.

Sometimes, we become insulted because our spouse disagrees with a value we hold important. In truth, there are always differences between two people who choose to spend their lives together. Exploring these differences enables generosity and peaceful diversity to grow. We can choose to either accept or to appreciate these differences. We can bless each other for our differences as well.

Negotiating takes practice. The outcome we are hoping to achieve is to establish peace, understanding, and curiosity about the differences between two people. In order to establish that, each person needs to master a number of skills. Negotiating is a set of skills that need to be learned and practiced so that two people can live together in peace and friendship while maintaining their right to individuality and growth. In a situation where there are no negotiations, one person typically must remain submissive, in an attempt to avoid conflict at all costs. Sometimes, this kind of relationship can work. However, for the most part, when two people decide to spend their lives together, they do so with the premise that they will both have the right to be individuals, with their own unique desires in life.

NEGOTIATING GONE RIGHT

My husband loves the beach. He would visit there every day, or even live there, if he could. I need the city for my work and my friends. Soon after we were married I realized that for him to be happy, I had to drop all my judgments about people and beaches. I was brought up believing that people who hang out on beaches were escaping life. My husband was not escaping; he was at peace on the beach. He enjoyed meeting people, and most of all, he felt happy with his life. In the end, we maintained our home in the suburbs, from where I could travel easily to the city, and even stay over whenever I needed to, and I also went with him to the beach, on occasion, and enjoyed the experience as well.

The skills needed for negotiation include:

- Taking turns speaking.
- Listening to the other person's ideas and requests.
- Approaching each negotiation with the idea that what is being expressed is important to the other person, even if you cannot see the importance of the request.
- Showing respect and patience.
- Being open to compromise.
- Entering each conversation with the understanding that there are two answers—"yes" or "no"—and both are valid.
- Knowing how to make new agreements.

Surprisingly, couples can actually grow closer through negotiations. They can learn to understand each other in a deeper way, and can learn sensitivity to the other person's ideas, even when there is no agreement.

It is a very limiting idea that two people can only be close if they agree on everything. Closeness and understanding can grow even when there is no agreement!

When the principles of respecting, seeking mutual benefit, and maintaining a relationship are placed ahead of any specific thorny issues, then negotiating can become an avenue for closeness and understanding, rather than an invitation for stress, conflict, and misunderstandings.

One important tip, however: In order to negotiate successfully, it is important to first be in a state of rapport and harmonious understanding with your partner. That will enable easier communication. Before you approach your partner to ask for something, think clearly about what you want and why you want it. Make sure you have calm feelings about the idea and breathe deeply before you begin!

PREPARATION FOR NEGOTIATION

Negotiation is essential to running a successful business, and using a business model can help us navigate negotiations in relationships. Before any negotiation takes place, a decision needs to be made as to when and where a meeting will take place to discuss the problem, as well as who will attend. Setting a limited time period can also help prevent disagreements from dragging on. Time limits create security in the face of a conversation that might create insecurity. Both people need to be given the opportunity to explain their reasoning, before they attempt to reach a decision. Stick to the facts and individual perceptions, and avoid insults and negative judgments at all costs. Negotiations need to be oriented toward finding solutions. Blame simply perpetuates conflict.

"Your constant yelling and swearing has made me feel sick every time I walk into our home," is a statement based on blame and judgment. This line of approach makes negotiation impossible, because no person accused like that will keep on listening. A better alternative would be, "I am experiencing too much yelling and swear words. I need a more peaceful home."

At this stage of negotiation, each side puts forth the case as they see it, expressing their understanding of the situation, and their hopes and preferences for change. These preferences should be expressed calmly, without threats or demands, as a simple hope for the future.

REACHING A POSITIVE OUTCOME

This stage of communication focuses on an outcome where both sides feel heard.

The sides then consider if a course of action can be formed that will take the first step toward change.

If the process of negotiation breaks down and agreement cannot be reached, then rescheduling a further meeting is another option. Rather than returning to blame and anger, rescheduling can be a way to say, "Nice try! It didn't work this time, but when should we speak again?" This prevents the couple from falling back into old patterns of heated discussions or arguments, which not only wastes time, but also damages their relationship.

When negotiating, it is better to speak in clear terms. Speaking clearly keeps both parties on the same page. If there is no understanding, it is important to be able to ask, "What does that mean?" Pretending to understand each other is a big invitation for alienation and misunderstanding. Collaboration comes when you know that each party understands the other.

Building rapport throughout the discussion can be done by speaking slowly, smiling whenever possible, and asking permission. Some effective phrases include: "Would it be possible...?" "Can we consider...?" and the like.

Good negotiation creates a spirit of freedom. This spirit is ensured by establishing at the beginning that both "yes" and "no" are acceptable answers. If negotiation becomes a false tactic to manipulate the outcome, the negotiation will fail. In a relationship and even in a business, negotiation is a process of growing closer *through* differences and complexities. It is not a tactic to get everything you want all the time, while ignoring the needs of the person on the other side of the table.

Although we adults are used to getting our way, having our preferences placed at the top of the list is actually a very small part of a successful relationship. The point of respectful negotiation is to take a complex part of a relationship and use it to grow closer, practice trusting each other, and come to understand that accommodating the other person's preference should also be considered a success, because it makes the relationship stronger. The opportunity for each person to express their ideas and choices is as important as the outcome of the negotiation itself. By listening to one's spouse's feelings and preferences, we come to understand them better and can be more sensitive, even when we disagree.

Negotiation is not only the best practice, it can be an expression of caring.

NEGOTIATION IN ACTION

Whenever I ask my husband for something like: "Can we go on a vacation this summer?" or, "Can we invite a friend to stay with us for a week?" he responds, "Let me think about it."

This used to drive me crazy! I felt I was asking for something reasonable, so why couldn't he just tell me his answer? When we learned negotiation skills, I realized this is how he reaches his decision. He needs time to think about things. He does not like to be pushed around, so he takes his time to fully understand what he thinks about a topic. Once I sensitized myself, I realized this was his style of negotiating—a style that I trust today!

SAMPLE NEGOTIATION 1

Wife: I've been thinking of stopping working and I'm wondering if it would be okay with you to support me for a while.

Husband: That would mean a lot of changes. You would have to be ready for them. I would need more control over our spending.

Wife: How much control would you need?

Husband: Well, I don't know. I just know it would have to be different.

Wife: But would I get to buy things?

Husband: Of course, but not everything you want. Not like now.

Wife: What do you think I buy now?

Husband: Well, like yesterday, you went to the health food store and the fruit store. Some things would have to change.

Wife: I wouldn't get to shop at the health food store?

Husband: We would need to rethink the whole organic produce thing. We would need to see how the expenses go.

Wife: Don't you want to eat organically?

Husband: Not if we can't afford it.

Wife: So, do you think it's a good idea? Do you think we could work it out?

Husband: I think it would be a hassle, but we could work it out in the end.

SAMPLE NEGOTIATION 2

Wife: Do you think you could tell me you love me more often?

Husband: I tell you I love you all the time.

Wife: I'm sorry. I don't mean to disagree, but you never say it unless I ask you if you love me. I want to know if you could tell me it without being asked.

Husband: I don't know what you're talking about. I know I say it a lot.

Wife: Should we keep track for a week, just to get a sense of this?

Husband: Okay. Keep track and I will, too, and we can compare notes next week.

AN EXERCISE: PRACTICING NEGOTIATION

Think of something you would like from your spouse to which you have no emotional attachment. Alternatively, find a topic you can discuss with your spouse, which you feel neutral or very secure about, such that it won't make a difference to you whether or not your spouse agrees with you. Ask for a time and a place to speak together.

When the time arrives, ask simply, clearly stating the reasons why having this thing is important to you. Or discuss the topic from your perspective and then let your spouse share their viewpoint.

See what happens. How do you feel at the end of the conversation? Ask your spouse how she or he feels, as well!

EPILOGUE

> So great is peace that God's name is peace, Shalom, and all the blessings are held within it.
>
> —*Shabbat* 10b; *Sifra, Bechukotai* 1:8

When your focus is on peace, the entire relationship changes. Peace is so important that it allows personal needs to take a back seat. And when personal needs are placed behind you, there is much more room for seeing the other person. Peace is like having a friend in the room, always bringing calmness and joy. Marriage is a golden opportunity for new growth in life, alone and as a couple.

THE NEXT STEP

I sincerely hope that this book has helped you in your life and relationships. If you would like to receive notifications of future volumes in this series, or occasional essays dedicated to helping you build meaningful and successful relationships, please write to:

Chana.frumin2@yahoo.com

* * *

If you enjoyed this book, I would be very grateful if you could leave a short online review. Online reviews help other people discover books that can aid them in their own lives, too.

ABOUT CHANA RACHEL FRUMIN

Chana Rachel Frumin has worked as a counselor for over forty years, and has practiced and taught narrative therapy for twenty of them. She has worked in numerous countries worldwide—including North America, South America, Africa, Australia, Europe, and Scandinavia—and has helped countless individuals overcome their personal and emotional challenges. She has supervised a clinic in Israel for the past twenty-two years, and, in Prague, for the past five years. She was a close student of Michael White, the founder of Narrative Therapy, for fifteen years and is presently a student of David Epston.

Her specialities include reclaiming life from the hand of trauma, beginning marriage from today, and finding new directions in life.

She has lived in Moshav Mevo Modi'in, Israel, for the last

forty years, and, together with her sweet husband, Zusha, has raised six wonderful children.

PRAISE FOR CHANA RACHEL FRUMIN

I have known Chana Rachel Frumin for over 25 years. While I was still a junior in experience and learning, Chana Rachel asked me to open a counseling center with her, which proved to be the formational years for me as a therapist. I had the opportunity to co-counsel with Mrs. Frumin and to learn her approach. She is a great therapist, who taught me how to combine my learned counseling skills with trust in my own intuition.

For both practicing therapists and students of growth, if you have had the good fortune to have found this book, do not pass up the opportunity to learn about and practice Chana Rachel's wisdom and humility. She combines the exceptional ability to be a master therapist with the humility to be a perpetual student. Her book is glimpse into the techniques she uses to teach and help people become the best versions of themselves.

—David Kaufman
Director of Outreach and Education at JACS
Canadian Certified Addiction Counselor
Nationally Certified Internet Addiction Coach

Drawing on over four decades of counseling experience and informed by a deep inner wisdom, Chana Rachel Frumin has presented a novel approach to marriage, relationships and fulfillment. An abundance of ideas and concepts, together with clear and penetrating examples from her therapeutic practice, make *The Pleasure of Peace* a valuable read, providing tools and inspiration to professional therapists and couples alike.

—Rabbi Chaim Tabasky
Director, Summer Program
Nishmat Seminary, Jerusalem

Transcending differences, instead of letting them divide a couple, is a crucial step towards rebuilding relationships. Chana Rachel's book taught me this is possible... and how to do it.

—Julie DeKoven,
MS Child Development, CNT
Child development cognitive counselor

Frumin offers a sophisticated and easy-to-apply approach to everyday relationships and interactions. Anyone who wants to understand both the complexities and ease of improving human behavior and communication will benefit from her insights.

—Peter Kline
International Educator
Author of *The Everyday Genius*

This book provides valuable insight into how to resolve problems in relationships using the authors own method called LEARN. Enjoy!

—Espen Thygesen
Norwegian Interdisciplinary Counselor

Chana Frumin's book has helped me look at my own marriage differently. I am now able to look my marital issues in a new, more hopeful light.

—D.S.

Made in the USA
Middletown, DE
04 July 2022